Your Complete Quinoa Recipe Guide
To Lose Weight, Boost Brain Power and Prevent Chronic Illness

SUPERFOOD SERIES BOOK 1

Copyright 2015 © Isabelle Matthews, RD

All Rights Reserved.

Disclaimer

All rights reserved. No part of this publication or the information in it may be quoted from or reproduced in any form by means such as printing, scanning, photocopying or otherwise without prior written permission of the copyright holder.

Effort has been made to ensure that the information in this book is accurate and complete, however, the author and the publisher do not warrant the accuracy of the information, text and graphics contained within the book due to the rapidly changing nature of science, research, known and unknown facts and the internet. The Author and the publisher do not hold any responsibility for errors, omissions or contrary interpretation of the subject matter herein. This book is presented solely for motivational and informational purposes only.

Introduction

The tiny grain-like seed, quinoa—pronounced "keen-wah"—finds itself, nearly 5,000 years after its initial cultivation, with a bit of celebrity. The Food and Agricultural Organization of the United Nations recently named the year 2013 "The International Year of the Quinoa," noting that the seed is an essential product, one with a high nutritive value. The United Nations declared that the seed must play an important part in creating food security all over the world—in areas where nutrition is bleak, where food is not as readily available.

This forces us to pay attention. There is something lurking beyond the hard coating of this rice-like seed. Recent studies have confirmed the fact that a diet high in quinoa can lead to decreased risk of cancers and heart disease via its high concentration of flavonoids called quercetin and kaempferol. Quinoa can also facilitate healthy weight loss by keeping us full as it provides high amounts of protein and fiber. Furthermore, quinoa provides heart-healthy fats, such as omega-3 fatty acids, that decrease your risk of heart disease and further boost brain productivity.

Quinoa, unfortunately, is not wildly utilized throughout much of North America at this time. It is unknown in a sea of breads, pastas, and rice. However, its elevated nutritional profile, extensive benefits, many different varieties, and its incredible ease when preparing fuel its vibrant recipes into many kitchens and many stomachs all over much of the world.

At the root of this book, of course, are the recipes. Find yourself preparing easy and delicious, quinoa-based breakfast recipes to incorporate a platform of nutrition for you to build from for the rest of the day. Note that the salad recipes are quite easy, prepared in just half an hour or so and can be utilized all throughout the week. Note further, that quinoa can be a hearty substitute for meat; it offers filling fiber, protein, fat, and carbohydrates to keep your brain going and to keep your cells healthy.

Read on to learn about the incredible history of quinoa, its nutritional profile, benefits, its many varieties and how to cook it properly. You will discover how truly healthy and tasty your life can be with this superfood, the quinoa seed.

Table of Contents

Chapter 1: A Brief History of Quinoa 9
Chapter 2: The Nutritional Background of Quinoa 13
Chapter 3: Ultimate Benefits of Quinoa 21
Chapter 4: Different Varieties of Quinoa 29
Chapter 5: Tips to Properly Cook Quinoa 33

Quinoa Breakfast Recipes 39
    Sun-Dried Tomato Quinoa-Stuffed Omelet 40
    Apple Walnut Quinoa Oatmeal 43
    Tropical Breakfast Coconut Quinoa 45
    Not-Your-Average Quinoa Hash Brown 47
    Spinach Quinoa Quiche 49
    Joyous Living Quinoa Pancakes 51

Quinoa Lunch Recipes 53
    Snap Peas and Asparagus Quinoa Lunch 54
    Red Quinoa Pistachio Delight 56
    Fennel-Based Quinoa and Pomegranate Dish 58
    Bacon, egg, and Quinoa Creation 60

Quinoa Dinner Recipes 63
    Winter's Day Sweet Potato and Quinoa Chili 64
    Quinoa and Pistachio-Stuffed Squash 66
    French-Style Quinoa and Chickpea Bajene 68
    Curry Quinoa with Indian-Inspired Cucumber
    Mint Dressing 71
    Super-Easy Quinoa Macaroni and Cheese 73
    Quinoa-Based Andes Burrito 75

Quinoa Salad Recipes 77
    Red and Green Radish Quinoa Salad 78
    Summertime Quinoa Tabbouleh 80

Light and Sweet Honeyed Quinoa Salad 82
Quinoa Carrot Salad with a Honey Glaze 84
Cauliflower-Walnut Red Quinoa Salad 87

Conclusion **89**

Chapter 1: A BRIEF HISTORY OF QUINOA

Quinoa, the nutritional-packed seed, finds its origins between 3,000 and 5,000 B.C. in the Andes Mountain, in the countries Peru, Bolivia, and Columbia. Quinoa was found smattered all over ancient tombs in Calama, Tarapaca, Chile, and Peru. We can therefore assume it held highest importance in the life of the Incans, the ancient South Americans. In fact, years ago, the emperor of the Incan land initiated the breaking of harvest ground utilizing a golden utensil to show his utmost respect for the quinoa seed and the life sustainment it offered. To this day, the seed is a mainstay in the Incan diet, toting the name "mother grain."

A few hundred years ago, when the European countries conquered South

America, the Spanish Colonists detested the mere thought of quinoa, viewing it only as the food for the Indians and not for their high-tier palates. They would not grow the seed; what's more, they actively suppressed its cultivation. The Spanish people began cultivating cereals, instead, and quinoa largely disappeared.

Fortunately, the Spanish were unsuccessful in killing the nutritional seed for good. In the 1980's, several thousand feet in the air on a Colorado mountain, two spiritual Americans who had visited and studied in the Bolivian Andes, the home of the quinoa seed, began cultivating quinoa once more.

After this rocky past—from mountain to mountain throughout the Americas—the quinoa seed was back and blossoming. The United Nations noted it as a 'superfood', declaring that it had the same protein count as milk. NASA added the quinoa seed to its all-important list of foods it would consider bringing into space for long-duration, continually manned flights.

And thusly: the quinoa seed is here to stay.

Chapter 2:
THE NUTRITIONAL BACKGROUND OF QUINOA

Andes-based quinoa plants are essential in any healthy diet. After all: quinoa is considered a superfood for a reason.

But let's breakdown what's actually in a cup of quinoa to better understand the intricate nutritional backdrop the mother seed offers.

Nutritional Breakdown for 1 cup Cooked Quinoa:

Calories: 222
Carbohydrates: 39 grams.
Protein: 8 grams.
Fat: 4 grams.
Manganese: 58% of your daily amount.
Fiber: 5 grams.

Magnesium: 30% of your daily amount.
Folate: 19% of your daily amount.
Phosphorus: 28% of your daily amount.
Iron: 15% of your daily amount.
Potassium: 9% of your daily amount.
Copper: 18% of your daily amount.
Zinc: 13% of your daily amount.
Vitamins B1, B2, and B6: over 10% of your daily amount.
Trace amounts of B3, Calcium, and Vitamin E.

Quinoa and Protein

Quinoa contains a high protein count, which is rare in the plant kingdom. Because it further boasts low-fat and a cholesterol-free elements, quinoa is an essential protein source for all vegans and vegetarians. Note that the recommended daily amount of protein a woman should consume is 46 grams, while the recommended daily amount for a man is around 55 grams.

Most impressively, quinoa brings all nine amino acids, which are the amino acids your body needs to re-fuel, grow new cells, and heal itself.

Quinoa and Iron

As you can see above, 15% of your recommended daily amount of iron is found in a single serving of quinoa. Iron is something we generally don't get enough of—especially if we're vegetarians, vegans, or people who like to stay away from red meat. Iron is an incredibly important element in the body. It works to transport red blood cells through the body and to deliver oxygen and other nutrients. Note that your cells need a continual intake of oxygen in order to stay alive and to stay healthy. Furthermore, iron is important in the creation of hormones, new cells, brain neurotransmitters, and many amino acids.

If you aren't getting enough iron, you may feel tired and be more prone to muscle soreness. Look to quinoa for a ready supply.

Quinoa and Manganese

As seen above, manganese is coursing through quinoa, providing you with 58% of your daily-recommended amount. In the past century, researchers have noted that we need manganese every single day in order to thrive and to keep our bodies healthy.

Role of Manganese

Essentially, manganese is important in bone development. Individuals who are deficient in manganese may be prone to weak bones and improper bone formation.

Furthermore, manganese triggers the activation of prolidase, an enzyme that creates collagen. Collagen gives your skin its spring and youthfulness. (We lose collagen as we get older.) Furthermore, manganese works to protect your skin against UV light and other irritants. A recent study noted that people who consumed low amounts of manganese over a period of several weeks developed rashes over their body. After returning to higher levels of manganese in their diet, their rashes disappeared.

Manganese further protects against free radicals. When you consume low levels of manganese, you're putting yourself at risk for cell death, cell-based inflammation, certain cancers, and heart disease.

In summery, manganese is one of the very essential reasons that quinoa is ranked one of the healthiest foods in the world.

Quinoa and Magnesium

Quinoa further offers 30% of your recommended daily dose of magnesium. Magnesium has a hand in many of your body's functions. For example, it is a co-factor (meaning it is a necessary element in the process) of over three hundred bodily enzymes. Furthermore, it allows your body to create protein, to control its blood glucose levels, and to regulate its blood pressure. It plays a vital role in the creation of DNA and RNA, as well; thusly, you would not be able to repair old cells or create new cells without the appropriate amount of magnesium.

Quinoa and Folate

19% of your daily-recommended amount of folate, or folic acid, is offered in each cup of quinoa.

Essentially, folic acid is necessary for everyone. However, it is most important that women between the ages of 11 to 49 intake an extra 400 micrograms of folate every single day. This is because folic acid prevents birth defects, whether you are currently pregnant or plan on becoming pregnant in the future.

Chapter 3:
ULTIMATE BENEFITS OF QUINOA

Quinoa was noted as a Superfood by the United Nations. After all, it packs hearty doses of fiber, protein, and many minerals. Alongside this extensive list of elements, quinoa doesn't contain a hint of gluten, an often-damaging wheat protein that has been deemed as a 'culprit' of inflammation in recent years in much of North America.

Look to the following health benefits of quinoa to learn how to assist your body on the path to weight loss, healing, and rejuvenation:

1. Quinoa Contains Cancer-Fighting Essential Flavonoids, Kaempferol and Quercetin.

Quinoa holds several vitamins and nutrients that boost your internal health and keep your cells working in top shape. Furthermore, quinoa contains elements called flavonoids, which are antioxidants that appear in plants. Note that flavonoids decrease inflammation on a cellular level and therefore put you at a decreased risk of developing certain diseases and cancers.

Two of these flavonoids are Quercetin and Kaempferol. These are found more densely packed in the tiny seeds of quinoa than in any other plant in the world. Working together, these flavonoids work against cancer development, inflammation, virus duplication, and depressive symptoms.

2. Quinoa Will Not Escalate Blood Sugar Levels Too Quickly

Note that a food's glycemic index measures how fast the blood sugar levels rise in the bloodstream. When you eat foods that have a high glycemic index, you can become hungry more quickly and you can put yourself at risk for both obesity and diabetes. Foods with high glycemic indexes include white bread, white pastas, and candy.

Quinoa, itself, has a glycemic index of 53. This is considered low on the glycemic index range.

Note, of course, that quinoa has a high carb content. Therefore, it should not be a staple in a low carbohydrate diet.

3. Quinoa contains All Essential Amino Acids for Healthy Muscle Growth

So often, vegetarians and vegans must formulate "complete" proteins by marrying different foods together, such as beans and rice. This is because rice "fills in" the missing amino acids in the beans, lending a complete protein.

Therefore, most plants are missing an essential amino acid; oftentimes, this amino acid is lysine.

Note, however, that quinoa contains lysine. It contains all of the amino acids, yielding complete proteins that do not have to be paired with anything to rev your metabolism and promote cell growth and rejuvenation.

4. Quinoa Can Boost Metabolic Health

Because quinoa is high in so many nutrients and vitamins, the seed has the capacity to improve your metabolic health.

A recent study noted that when people began replacing all their gluten-free breads and pastas with quinoa, their insulin, blood sugar, and triglyceride levels decreased dramatically. Note that decreasing these numbers is the key to halting metabolic syndrome and improving your health.

Furthermore, it's important to note that if your diet is high in fructose, quinoa can eliminate the harmful effects of the fruit-based sugar. You can have your fibrous fruits without receiving the negative backdrop of the fruit's sugar.

5. Quinoa Can Facilitate Weight Loss

At the root of all weight loss endeavors, it is essential that we take in fewer calories than we burn. However, this exchange can become a bit more complicated. For example, some properties in certain types of food can boost your metabolism, thus increasing the number of calories you burn. Alternately, some foods can decrease your appetite, thus allowing you to take in fewer calories.

Quinoa is pulsing with many of these positive properties.

It is very high in protein, for one, which both revs your metabolism and decreases your appetite.

Furthermore, it's high in fiber, which has been proven to help you eat fewer and fewer calories. It moves slowly through your digestive system and makes you feel fuller for longer.

In addition, quinoa's low glycemic index works to decrease your overall "need' for junk foods. Therefore, eating quinoa can trick your mind into not wanting more sweets or more carb-loaded foods.

As you can see, quinoa can bring vitamins, minerals, nutrients, proteins, and fiber that can put your body in the appropriate environment for weight loss.

Chapter 4: Different Varieties of Quinoa

Many different types of quinoa are available all over the Andes. However, in the rest of the world, three types of quinoa are readily available: white quinoa, red quinoa, and black quinoa. Furthermore, you can find altered quinoa: quinoa flakes and quinoa flour, both often used for baking purposes.

Read below for more information.

White Quinoa

White quinoa is the most popular type of quinoa. Oftentimes, in stores, white quinoa (or golden quinoa) is simply referred to as "quinoa." This white quinoa has the lightest texture. When it cooks, it fluffs up much more easily. Furthermore, its taste is delicate. It pairs well with almost everything, and it can serve as a good substitute for rice.

White quinoa takes just fifteen to seventeen minutes to cook.

Red Quinoa

Red quinoa, when cooked, turns a bit brown. It's rich, more vibrant than its white cousin. Furthermore, it's chewier and a bit nuttier. Generally, it's most often used for cold salads. This is because it keeps its shape much more easily.

Purple quinoa, sometimes found in stores, has many red quinoa characteristics. Orange quinoa is similar to red quinoa, as well; however, it is a bit milder, lacking in flavor.

Red, purple, and orange quinoa requires approximately seventeen to twenty minutes to cook.

Black Quinoa

Black quinoa is the "sweet" one. It's a bit earthy, as well, with a crunchier texture. It holds it shape much better than white quinoa; therefore, it can be utilized for cold dishes, like salads.

Black quinoa requires approximately twenty to twenty-three minutes to cook.

Quinoa Flakes

Quinoa flakes are created much like rolled oats or barley flakes. The seed is steamrolled to create the flakes. Note that these flakes cook much more quickly than the general seed. They are appropriate for baking or a quick breakfast.

Quinoa Flour

Quinoa flour is often turned to for healthful baking opportunities. You can find it at a local health food store. Alternately, you can make it at home by grinding white quinoa in a coffee grinder until it is a fine powder.

Chapter 5:
TIPS TO PROPERLY COOK QUINOA

Quinoa's popularity is bursting everywhere. Its delightful, light texture and its high protein content have made it a mainstay in kitchens and restaurants alike. But how do you cook it to its proper fluffy consistency, without mushing it or making it bitter?

Note the following basic facts of cooking quinoa before getting started:

1. Dry quinoa to cooked quinoa: What's the yield?

1 cup of dry quinoa seeds creates 3 cups of cooked quinoa.

2. Dry quinoa and cooking liquid: How much do I need?

In order to cook one cup of quinoa, you require 2 cups of liquid. Utilize either broth or water.

3. Cooking quinoa: How much time do I need?

You should be able to cook 1 cup of quinoa in just twenty minutes. Black quinoa takes a few minutes longer.

4. Cooking quinoa: How to eliminate the bitterness

The outer coating of quinoa garners a bit of bitterness. You can remove this easily simply by rinsing the quinoa in a mesh strainer prior to cooking.

5. How do I liven up the taste of my quinoa?

Note that many people are disinterested in cooking their quinoa in water. This is because, generally, the fluffy grain tastes a bit bland without adding something else to it. Therefore, you can cook the quinoa in vegetable or chicken broth, add a bit of salt during the cooking process, and experiment with rosemary, garlic, or black pepper. There's a world of opportunity when experimenting with quinoa flavors. The quinoa seed offers a backdrop of nutrition, ready to soak up all the flavors you enjoy.

6. Do rice cookers prepare quinoa properly?

Of course! Just as listed above, you only require a 2:1 ratio of liquid to quinoa, even in the rice cooker.

Learn to Properly Rinse Quinoa

Note that, traditionally, you must properly rinse quinoa before you cook it. This is because quinoa seeds are coated with something called saponin. This is a bitter protectant that keeps the seed alive in the wild, away from predators.

However, many brands of quinoa sold throughout North America sell their quinoa pre-washed. In order to remove the saponin yourself, do the following steps:

1. Pour the quinoa into a bowl.
2. Cover the quinoa with water.
3. Allow the quinoa to sit for two minutes before swishing it around.
4. After swishing it, drain the quinoa in a fine-mesh sieve.

Steps to Cook Quinoa Perfectly, Every Time

Quinoa is similar to rice and pasta. All you need is water and some heat. The most simplistic way to cook quinoa is found here:

1. Begin by pouring 1 cup of quinoa with 2 cups of water (or broth) in a medium-sized saucepan.
2. Bring the water (or broth) to boil.
3. When the water begins to boil, reduce the heat to low.
4. Cover the saucepan and allow the quinoa to simmer for approximately fifteen to twenty minutes.
5. Drain out the rest of the water and return the quinoa to the saucepan.
6. Cover the saucepan once more and allow the quinoa to sit for five minutes.
7. After five minutes, fluff the quinoa with your fork prior to serving.

Sun-dried Tomato Quinoa-Stuffed Omelet

Recipe Makes 2 Servings.

Nutritional Breakdown Per Serving: 319 calories, 9 grams carbohydrates, 26 grams protein, 19 grams fat.

Ingredients:
6 eggs
1 tsp. olive oil
1 tsp. butter
1 diced onion
4 minced garlic cloves
1/3 cup sliced sun-dried tomatoes
1/3 cup cooked quinoa
3 large handfuls baby spinach
½ tsp. red pepper flakes
1/3 cup goat cheese
Salt and pepper to taste

Directions:
Begin by cracking each of the eggs into a small mixing bowl, whisking them together, and setting them to the side.

Next, heat the olive oil in a skillet over medium-high. Allow the onions to cook in the oil for about five minutes, stirring occasionally. Next, add the tomatoes, red pepper flakes, and garlic. Stir for an additional minute before adding the spinach, just one bit at a time.

Cook this mixture until the greens begins to wilt. Salt and pepper the mixture as you please, and transfer the mixture to a bowl, away from the heat.

Next, melt the butter in a skillet over medium-high temperature. Pour half of the egg mixture into this pan. As the bottom begins to set, utilize a spatula to lift up the sides. Cook until the top is set and the bottom is golden.

Next, administer half of the spinach mixture overtop one half of the omelet. Add half of the quinoa over this filling, and then add half of the goat cheese over the quinoa.

Fold over the omelet, and then slide the omelet onto your plate. Repeat all the above steps with your next omelet, and enjoy.

Apple Walnut Quinoa Oatmeal

Recipe Makes 1 Serving.

Nutritional Breakdown per Serving: 440 calories, 70 grams carbohydrates, 15 grams protein, 13 grams fat.

Ingredients:
1/3 cup red quinoa
1/3 cup oats
1 cup boiling water
1/3 cup almond milk
½ tsp. cinnamon
1 ½ tbsp. diced walnuts
½ shredded apple
½ tsp. salt

Directions:
Begin by rinsing out the quinoa and draining it well. Mix together the quinoa and the oats in a small saucepan, and cover the mixture with a cup of boiling water.

Next, bring this mixture to a boil. When it begins to boil, add the cinnamon, almond milk, and salt. Reduce the heat, and cook, stirring off and on, for about ten minutes.

Preheat the oven to 350 degrees Fahrenheit. Toast the diced walnuts in a baking sheet, making sure to stir occasionally. Do this for about four minutes.

Once the quinoa and oats have incorporated much of the water, pour it into a bowl and top it with walnuts and apple. Add more cinnamon if desired, and enjoy.

Tropical Breakfast Coconut Quinoa

Recipe Makes 6 Servings.

Nutritional Breakdown Per Serving: 353 calories, 33 grams carbohydrates, 8 grams protein, 22 grams fat.

Ingredients:
1 ¾ cup rinsed quinoa
1 ½ tbsp. coconut oil
1 can coconut milk, unsweetened
1 ½ cups water
½ tsp. salt

Directions:
Begin by heating the coconut oil in a saucepan over medium. At this time, add the quinoa and stir often until it turns golden. This should take about five minutes. Next, add coconut milk, salt, and water, stirring well. Allow the water to boil before reducing the heat to low, covering the pot, and allowing the ingredients to simmer for twenty-five minutes.

Allow the quinoa to sit for ten minutes before fluffing and serving. Enjoy!

Not-Your-Average Quinoa Hash Browns

Recipe Makes 2 Servings.

Nutritional Breakdown Per Serving: 294 calories, 34 grams carbohydrates, 9 grams protein, 13 grams fat.

Ingredients:
1 cup water
½ cup quinoa
1 egg
1 1/3 cup grated potato
½ tsp. sea salt
½ tsp. pepper
1 ½ tbsp. butter
2 diced green onions

Directions:
Begin by bringing the water and the quinoa together in a saucepan. Allow the water to boil. After it begins to boil, cover the saucepan and allow the quinoa to simmer on LOW for ten minutes. After ten minutes, turn off the heat. Allow the saucepan to remain on the hot burner for

seven additional minutes with the cover still on. Fluff up the mixture with your fork.

Next, stir together the quinoa, egg, potato, green onions and salt and pepper. Heat up a skillet and melt the butter over medium-high heat.

Next, scoop out a third of a cup of the quinoa potato mixture and flatten it into a patty in the skillet over the butter. Cook the hash brown patties for seven minutes on each side, making sure to make them golden. Repeat with your remaining hash brown mixture, and enjoy!

Spinach Quinoa Quiche

Recipe Makes 4 Servings.

Nutritional Breakdown Per Serving: 347 calories, 33 grams carbohydrates, 23 grams protein, 13 grams fat.

Ingredients:
1 cup cooked quinoa
400 grams frozen spinach, (thaw in the refrigerator overnight)
1 ¼ cup ricotta cheese
1 tsp. garlic salt
3 eggs
1 cup Parmesan cheese

Directions:
Begin by preheating your oven to 350 degrees Fahrenheit.

Next, allow the quinoa to simmer in a pot of boiling water for approximately fifteen minutes before draining it and allowing it to cool for a few minutes in the covered pot.

Mix together cooked quinoa, spinach, eggs, ricotta, Parmesan and garlic salt. Pour this mixture into a baking dish, and position the baking dish in the preheated oven.

Allow the quiche to cook for forty-five minutes. Afterwards, remove the quiche and allow it to cool for a few minutes. Slice and serve. Enjoy!

Joyous Living Quinoa Pancakes

Recipe Makes 8 Servings.

Nutritional Breakdown Per Serving: 300 calories, 44 grams carbohydrates, 8 grams protein, 9 grams fat.

Ingredients:
1 ¾ cup all-purpose flour
2 tsp. baking powder
1/3 cup quinoa flour
½ cup coconut sugar
2 cups 2% milk
3 separated eggs
1 tsp. vanilla
2 cups cooked quinoa
4 tbsp. melted butter
1/3 cup applesauce
1 ¼ cup blueberries

Directions:
Begin by mixing together the quinoa flour and the all-purpose flour in a mixing bowl. Add salt, coconut sugar, baking powder, and stir well.

To the side, separate the egg yolks from the egg whites in two separate bowls. To the yolk bowl, add milk, applesauce, butter, and vanilla. Stir well, and then add the dry ingredients—flour, sugar, etc. Continue to stir.

To the side, beat the egg whites to create soft peaks. Add this to the pre-created mixture, and stir. At this time, add the quinoa.

To the side, preheat a griddle. Drop a fourth cup of batter onto the griddle. As the batter sets on the griddle, drop on a few blueberries. Flip the pancake when the bottom is brown. Cook until the second side is browned. Position all the pancakes on a plate, and enjoy with maple syrup!

QUINOA
LUNCH
RECIPES

Snap Pea and Asparagus Quinoa Lunch

Recipe Makes 4 Servings.

Nutritional Breakdown Per Serving: 570 calories, 75 grams carbohydrates, 23 grams protein, 15 grams fat.

Ingredients:
4 cups water
1 tbsp. olive oil
2 cups rinsed quinoa
1 tsp. sea salt
1 lemon
1 cup snap peas
1/3 pound sliced and diced asparagus
1 can chickpeas
1 ½ tbsp. chopped chives
1/3 cup sliced radishes
1/3 cup crumbled goat cheese

Directions:
Begin by heating olive oil and water together in a saucepan over medium heat. Allow the water to boil. Salt the water and add the quinoa. Stir well and return to

boil. Next, turn the heat to low and allow the quinoa to simmer, with the cover over it, for twenty minutes. After twenty minutes, remove the quinoa from the heat and set it to the side for fifteen minutes, keeping the cover overtop.

To the side, heat 4 cups of water in a large pot. Salt the water. To the side, prepare a bath of ice water.

Toss the snap peas and the asparagus into the boiling water. Cook the vegetables for four minutes. At this time, drain out the vegetables and place them in the cold water immediately. This way, they'll stay nice and crunchy.

To the side, zest the lemon and squeeze out the juice into a small bowl. After the quinoa is completely cooked, add the vegetables, chickpeas, radishes, lemon zest, lemon juice, chives, and parsley to a large bowl with the quinoa. Add goat cheese overtop, and enjoy.

Red Quinoa Pistachio Delight

Recipe Makes 4 Servings.

Nutritional Breakdown Per Serving: 314 calories, 41 grams carbohydrates, 10 grams protein, 12 grams fat.

Ingredients:
1 diced shallot
1 tbsp. olive oil
½ tsp. sea salt
1 ¼ cup rinsed, red quinoa
2 cups chicken broth or water
1/3 cup diced pistachios
4 tbsp. chopped parsley
2 tbsp. chopped mint

Directions:
Begin by heating the olive oil in a saucepan over medium. Add the shallot and cook for about five minutes, stirring occasionally. Add the quinoa and cook for an additional five minutes, making sure the quinoa begins to toast.

Add the chicken broth or water to the mixture at this point, and bring the mixture to a boil.

When the water begins to boil, reduce the heat to low, place the cover on the pot, and simmer the quinoa for thirty minutes. Remove the pot from the heat and fluff the quinoa with your fork. Cover the pot and allow it to stand for an additional five minutes.

Add the mint, parsley, and the pistachios to the mixture. Salt and pepper to taste, and enjoy.

Fennel-Based Quinoa and Pomegranate Dish

Recipe Makes 4 Servings.

Nutritional Breakdown Per Serving: 332 calories, 33 grams carbohydrates, 7 grams protein, 19 grams fat.

Ingredients:
2 ½ sliced fennel bulbs
1/3 cup olive oil
2 tsp. cumin
2 ½ tbsp. lemon juice
1 lemon
1 tsp. sugar
1 ¼ cup rinsed quinoa
3 cups water
1 diced chili pepper
1/3 cup chopped cilantro
1/3 cup pomegranate seeds

Directions:
Begin by heating olive oil in a skillet over medium. Add fennel and cook it for approximately twelve minutes. Add lemon juice, sugar, and cumin to the

fennel and cook for one minute more. Set the skillet off to the side.

Next, pour 3 cups of water and the rinsed quinoa into a saucepan. Allow it to boil over medium-high. When it begins to boil, cover the saucepan and reduce the heat to low. Allow the quinoa to simmer for twelve minutes. After twelve minutes, drain the quinoa and then return it to the pot. Cover the pot and allow it to rest for seventeen minutes before fluffing at it with your fork and positioning it in a large serving bowl.

To the side, peel and chop the lemon. Add the lemon membrane and juices to the quinoa. Stir well. Next, add the fennel, herbs, and the chili pepper. Toss the mixture well before seasoning with salt and pepper.

Add the pomegranate seeds overtop, and enjoy!

Bacon, Egg, and Quinoa Creation

Recipe Makes 6 Servings.

Nutritional Breakdown Per Serving: 519 calories, 51 grams carbohydrates, 16 grams protein, 28 grams fat.

Ingredients:
6 slices diced bacon
1/3 cup lemon juice
1 ½ tbsp. red wine vinegar
2 minced garlic cloves
1 ½ tsp. Dijon mustard
1/3 cup olive oil
1 tsp. honey
1 ¾ cup watercress sprigs
2 ¾ cup cooked quinoa
1 peeled and pitted avocado
2 peeled and diced hard-boiled eggs
1/3 cup crumbled feta cheese
1 diced tomato

Directions:
Begin by cooking the bacon in a skillet until it's crispy; this should take about eight minutes.

Next, transition the bacon to a paper towel.

To the side, mix together vinegar, Dijon, lemon juice, honey, and garlic in a mixing bowl. Add the oil slowly. Season this dressing with salt and pepper, if you desire.

Next, position the watercress sprigs out on a large serving platter. Add the bacon, cooked quinoa, hard-boiled eggs, tomato, avocado, and the feta cheese overtop. Pour the dressing over the entire creation, and enjoy!

QUINOA DINNER RECIPES

Winter's Day Sweet Potato and Quinoa Chili

Recipe Makes 6 Servings.

Nutritional Breakdown Per Serving: 330 calories, 57 grams carbohydrates, 15 grams protein, 5 grams fat,

Ingredients:
1 diced onion
1 tbsp. olive oil
14 ounces roasted tomatoes
5 cups water
6 minced garlic cloves
2 tbsp. chili powder
½ tbsp. coriander
½ pound rinsed and uncooked, dried black beans
1 tsp. oregano
1/3 cup rinsed and drained quinoa
3 cubed sweet potatoes

Directions:
Begin by heating the olive oil in the bottom of a large chili pot over medium heat. Next, cook the onion for eight

minutes. Toss in the garlic, coriander, chili powder, and stir well for one additional minute.

Next, add the tomatoes, dried beans, and the oregano. Pour in five cups of water, and allow the water to come to a boil. At this time, reduce the heat to low, cover the pot, and allow the mixture to simmer between two and four hours. (Note that this depends on how old your dried beans are.)

After approximately ninety minutes, toss in the quinoa, sweet potatoes, and a bit of salt. Continue cooking for an additional 30 minutes, adding a bit more water if the chili becomes too thick.

Enjoy the chili warm. Note that you can freeze it, if you like, to enjoy at a later date.

Quinoa and Pistachio-Stuffed Squash

Recipe Makes 3 Servings.

Nutritional Breakdown Per Serving: 115 calories, 7 grams carbohydrates, 3 grams protein, 9 grams fat.

Ingredients:
3 squashes (I used sweet dumpling)
1 diced onion
1 tbsp. olive oil
1/3 cup chopped pistachios
1 ½ tsp. lemon zest
10 chopped dates
1 cup cooked quinoa
1 tsp. cinnamon
Salt and pepper to taste

Directions:
Begin by preheating the oven to 375 degrees Fahrenheit.

Next, slice the squash into halves and remove the seeds.

Position the squashes with their faces down on a baking dish. Bake the squash for about thirty minutes, or until they are tender. Remove the squash, keeping the oven at the 375 degree temperature.

Next, heat olive oil in a saucepan over medium. Sauté the onion until it's clear, and then add the dates, pistachios, cinnamon, and the lemon zest. Cook for another two minutes before adding the pre-cooked quinoa. Season with salt and pepper.

Next, stuff the squash with stuffing and cover the baking dish with aluminum foil. Bake for twenty minutes before serving warm.

Enjoy!

French-Style Quinoa and Chickpea Bajene

Recipe Makes 4 Servings.

Nutritional Breakdown Per Serving: 350 calories, 59 grams carbohydrates, 11 grams protein, 7 grams fat.

Ingredients:

For the Quinoa:
1 ¼ cup dried, rinsed quinoa
2 tsp. olive oil
3 minced garlic cloves
1 ¼ cup water
2 tsp. chopped thyme
½ tsp. sea salt

For the Chickpeas:
2 ½ cups sliced leeks
2 tsp. olive oil
2 cups sliced carrots
2 cups sliced fennel
1/3 cup white wine
1 ¼ cup vegetable broth
5 minced garlic cloves

14 ounces chickpeas from a can
5 tsp. chopped thyme
½ tbsp. lemon juice
5 ounces baby spinach

Directions:

Begin by utilizing the quinoa ingredients. Heat olive oil in a saucepan over medium-high heat. Add the garlic to the saucepan and allow it to cook for one minute. At this time, add water, quinoa, thyme, and salt, stirring well. Cover the saucepan, reduce the heat to low, and allow the quinoa to simmer for fifteen minutes.

Next, work from the chickpea list. Heat the olive oil in a large Dutch oven on medium-high. Add garlic and leeks, and allow them to cook for six minutes. Next, add the fennel and the carrots. Sauté for an additional 12 minutes. Pour the white wine into the pot and cook for an additional three minutes. Add the vegetable broth along with half of the thyme and the chickpeas. Cook for two more minutes before removing it from the heat and adding lemon juice, spinach, and some salt and pepper.

Next, prepare the meal by placing a bit of quinoa in four different bowls. Top each of the bowls with the chickpea mixture. Add the remaining thyme overtop, and enjoy.

Curry Quinoa with an Indian-Inspired Cucumber Mint Dressing

Recipe Makes 6 Servings.

Nutritional Breakdown Per Serving: 270 calories, 45 grams carbohydrates, 10 grams protein, 4 grams fat.

Ingredients:
2 ¼ cup water
1 tsp. olive oil
1 ¼ cup rinsed quinoa
3 minced garlic cloves
1 diced and peeled mango
1 tsp. salt
2 ½ tsp. curry powder
¾ cup diced celery
4 tbsp. currants
4 tbsp. chopped cilantro
2 tsp. diced mint
1/3 cup diced and peeled cucumber
6 ounces low-fat yogurt, plain
5 ounces baby spinach

Directions:

Begin by heating olive oil in a saucepan over medium-high. Next, add garlic and curry to the pan and cook them together for two minutes, stirring all the time. Add the water and the quinoa and bring the mixture to a boil. Cover the saucepan and reduce the heat, allowing the quinoa to simmer for seventeen minutes. Remove the quinoa from the heat and allow it to cool to room temperature.

Net, add the celery, mango, green onions, currants, and the cilantro to the quinoa, and toss the quinoa mixture to combine everything.

To the side, mix together the cucumber, mint, and yogurt. Stir well.

Next, divide the spinach between six plates. Top the spinach with the quinoa. Then, top the quinoa with the created "raita" or cucumber, yogurt dressing.

Super-Easy Quinoa Macaroni and Cheese

Recipe Makes 6 Servings.

Nutritional Breakdown Per Serving: 410 calories, 60 grams carbohydrates, 17 grams protein, 10 grams fat.

Ingredients:
1 butternut squash
1 ½ tbsp. Dijon mustard
1/3 cup almond milk
3 ½ cups cooked quinoa
¾ cup cheddar cheese, shredded

Directions:
Begin by preheating your oven to 375 degrees Fahrenheit.

Next, peel the squash and remove the seeds. Slice and dice the butternut squash into small, one-inch sized chunks. Add the squash to a large soup pot, cover the squash with about an inch of water, and boil the squash for approximately seventeen minutes. At this time, drain the squash and add the pieces to a blender.

Next, pour the almond milk and the mustard into the blender with the squash. Blend on high until the mixture is smooth. Add additional milk as needed.

Next, pour this mixture into a serving bowl. Add the quinoa and the shredded cheese. Stir the mixture until it's combined.

Next, pour this mixture into a baking dish. Add the macaroni to the oven and cook it for thirty minutes. It should be bubbly on top.

Remove the macaroni from the oven, allow it to cool, and enjoy!

Quinoa-Based Andes Burrito

Recipe Makes 8 Servings.

Nutritional Breakdown Per Serving: 650 calories, 80 grams carbohydrates, 33 grams protein, 21 grams fat.

Ingredients:
1 ¼ cup rinsed quinoa
1 diced onion
2 ½ tbsp. olive oil
2 ½ tsp. chili powder
1 cup vegetable broth
30 ounces canned pinto beans
20 ounces thawed, frozen spinach—squeezed of excess water
3 minced garlic cloves
3 cups shredded cheddar cheese
8 tortillas, for wrapping

Directions:
Begin by heating the oven to 400 degrees Fahrenheit.

At this time, boil a pot of water and then add the quinoa. Allow the quinoa to simmer for approximately fifteen minutes.

To the side, heat olive oil in a skillet and cook the onion for five minutes. Toss in the chili powder and cook for an additional minute.

Next, pour the beans, garlic, and broth into this skillet and allow the mixture to simmer, stirring occasionally. The liquid should be absorbed. Add the spinach.

Next, portion the quinoa, the bean mix, and the cheddar into each tortilla. Roll the burritos and then wrap them in aluminum foil.

Position each burrito on the baking sheet. Bake the burritos for fifteen minutes. Afterwards, serve warm with toppings of your choice. Enjoy!

Red and Green Radish Quinoa Salad

Recipe Makes 2 Servings.

Nutritional Breakdown Per Serving: 320 calories, 29 grams carbohydrates, 7 grams protein, 20 grams fat.

Ingredients:
1/3 cup quinoa
4 tbsp. butter
1 cup water
2 cups spinach
¾ cup sliced radishes
1 tsp. lemon juice
1 ½ tsp. lemon zest
2 tbsp. chopped fresh basil
½ tsp. sea salt

Directions:
Begin by rinsing and draining the quinoa. Pour the uncooked quinoa in a saucepan along with a cup of water and the butter. Bring the mixture to a boil before covering it and allowing it to simmer on low.

Allow the mixture to simmer for approximately twenty minutes, until the water has disappeared.

Next, remove the saucepan from the heat and allow it to stand for ten minutes. Fluff it up with your fork.

At this time, toss the quinoa with the other ingredients, mixing well. Add salt, if desired.

Enjoy!

Summertime Quinoa Tabbouleh

Recipe Makes 10 Servings.

Nutritional Breakdown Per Serving: 230 calories, 19 grams carbohydrates, 8 grams protein, 14 grams fat.

Ingredients:
1 cup dry quinoa
2 cups water
2 cups chopped, fresh parsley
1 diced onion
2 diced tomatoes
1 bunch chopped mint
3 tbsp. lemon juice
1/3 cup olive oil
3 minced garlic cloves
Salt and pepper to taste

Directions:
Begin by rinsing out the quinoa and bringing the quinoa, two cups of water, and a pinch of salt together in a saucepan. Allow the water to simmer before positioning the heat to medium-low.

Cover the pot and cook for about twenty minutes, until the quinoa with fluffy.

To the side, as the quinoa cooks, soak the onion in cold water to soften it.

Next, pour the cooked quinoa in a large mixing bowl and allow it to cool. To the side, drain out the onions, and then add the onions to the quinoa along with parsley, mint, tomatoes, and garlic. Stir together olive oil and the lemon juice, and add this to the quinoa, as well, stirring well.

Serve the salad a few hours after to allow the ingredients to mingle. Enjoy!

Light and Sweet Honeyed Quinoa Salad

Recipe Makes 8 Servings.

Nutritional Breakdown Per Serving: 200 calories, 23 grams carbohydrates, 4 grams protein, 11 grams fat.

Ingredients:
1 cup rinsed quinoa
1 ½ cubed sweet potatoes
5 tsp. apple cider vinegar
¼ cup pine nuts
4 tbsp. olive oil, divided
2 ½ tsp. honey
½ tsp. cumin
½ tsp. cinnamon
½ tsp. pepper
¼ cup raisins

Directions:
Begin by preheating the oven to 400 degrees Fahrenheit.

To the side, pour the quinoa in a saucepan with 2 cups of water. Allow the water to boil and then simmer for twenty minutes. Afterwards, turn off the heat and allow the quinoa to sit in the saucepan for one hour with the cover overtop.

Next, roast the sweet potatoes with 1 tbsp. of olive oil in the preheated oven for twenty-five minutes. Set these to the side.

Next, place the pine nuts in a small skillet and heat them until they're toasted, stirring all the time. Set these to the side.

In a small bowl, pour the remaining olive oil, honey, vinegar, cumin, cinnamon, salt, and pepper. Stir well.

After the quinoa has rested for one hour, pour the quinoa in a large mixing bowl. Add the created vinaigrette and stir. Next, add the sweet potatoes, raisins, and pine nuts, stirring well. Serve and enjoy!

Quinoa Carrot Salad with a Honey Glaze

Recipe Makes 4 Servings.

Nutritional Breakdown Per Serving: 430 calories, 55 grams carbohydrates, 8 grams protein, 20 grams fat.

Ingredients:
1 diced onion
1 ¼ cup rinsed quinoa
4 cups water
1/3 cup olive oil
3 tbsp. honey
3 tbsp. apple cider
4 peeled and sliced carrots
1 ½ tbsp. apple cider vinegar
1 tbsp. lemon juice
3 tbsp. lemon zest
1/3 cup sliced pickled beets
1 head shredded lettuce

Directions:
Begin by preheating your oven to 450 degrees Fahrenheit.

Pour the quinoa into a saucepan along with 4 cups of water. Bring the water to a boil. When it begins to boil, cover the saucepan and allow it to simmer for about fifteen minutes. At this time, add the onion to the mixture and cook for an additional three minutes.

Next, drain the saucepan and then return the quinoa and onion to the saucepan. Allow the quinoa to sit, covered, for an additional fifteen minutes before fluffing at it with a fork. Transfer the quinoa to a large mixing bowl.

To the side, coat a large baking sheet with oil. To the side, stir together the cider and the honey. Add salt and pepper. Add the carrots to this mixture and toss them. Transfer the carrots to the baking sheet and roast them for twenty minutes.

To the side, whisk together lemon zest, lemon juice, and the vinegar in a little bowl. Add the olive oil to the bowl, stirring slowly to blend well.

Next, add the beets, carrots, and the vinaigrette to the quinoa and toss the quinoa well. Add the lettuce to the quinoa and toss well once more before serving. Enjoy!

Cauliflower-Walnut Red Quinoa Salad

Recipe Makes 6 Servings.

Nutritional Breakdown Per Serving: 300 calories, 17 grams carbohydrates, 5 grams protein, 25 grams fat.

Ingredients:
½ grated head of cauliflower
½ cup pitted olives
¾ cup red quinoa
½ cup chopped parsley
½ cup chopped walnuts
½ cup olive oil
1 tsp. cumin
2 tbsp. lemon juice
2 tsp. lemon zest

Directions:
Begin by allowing a large pot of water to boil. When it begins to boil, add the quinoa and allow it to simmer for fifteen minutes. At this time, drain the quinoa and then return it to the pot. Cover the pot and allow the quinoa to stand for ten

minutes before fluffing it with your fork. Pour the quinoa into a large serving bowl.

Mix together the quinoa with the other ingredients: cauliflower, olives, parsley, walnuts, olive oil, cumin, lemon juice, and lemon zest. Season with salt and pepper, and serve. Enjoy!

Conclusion

The Quinoa Cookbook brings quinoa, the often-mispronounced new "superfood," into new understanding. Discovered so long ago growing wildly in the Incan mountains, the original people of the earth turned to it for sustenance and for well-being. After hundreds of years, quinoa has burst into the twenty-first century to bring us relief from the western diet that continually kills us, every single day. The quinoa superfood offers nutrients, vitamins, complete proteins, good, heart-healthy fats, and so much more to fuel a lifestyle that supports graceful aging, weight loss, and happiness. With quinoa, we can truly allow our food to be our medicine, like the old Greek saying.

Furthermore, this cookbook offers extensive recipes that feature quinoa as their main ingredient. If you like the classic macaroni and cheese but want the nutritional backing and protein of the quinoa seed, you have it here. If you want to eat quinoa for breakfast, thus stocking yourself with filling fiber that will stick with you the rest of the day, you have it. The salad recipes are vibrant; the chili recipe is perfect for the winter months and rainy days. Quinoa is appropriate for every single day of the year. Your body—void of nutrients and vitamins it requires to stay healthy—yearns for a superfood like quinoa. Give your body what it needs to help you live the best life you can.

Made in the USA
Lexington, KY
20 January 2016